ALL THINGS WHALES FOR KIDS

FILLED WITH PLENTY OF FACTS, PHOTOS, AND
FUN TO LEARN ALL ABOUT WHALES

ANIMAL READS

WWW.ANIMALREADS.COM

THIS BOOK BELONGS TO...

_____

_____

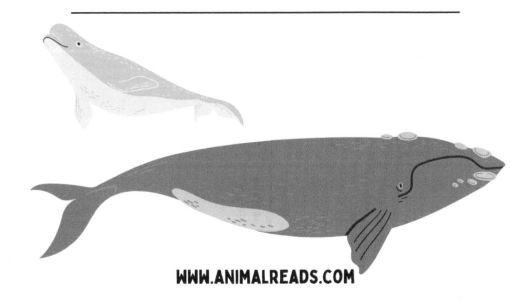

CONTENTS

WELCOME TO THE GINORMOUS WORLD OF WHALES

Whales are among the most loved and mysterious creatures on our planet. These gentle sea giants have captivated our imagination for hundreds ...**no, make that, *thousands* of years.** Their sheer gargantuan size leaves humans in awe. Their ability to live and thrive in some of the world's most inhospitable regions, like the waters of the Arctic and the Antarctic, is just one of the many reasons people find whales so incredibly fascinating.

Perhaps you have been lucky enough to have seen a whale on a very special boat trip. If you haven't, don't worry, you'll still have plenty of time to travel the world in search of these extraordinary creatures. And even if you have: seeing one whale is *not* seeing all the whales.

Our planet is home to about 90 distinct species of whales. Among them, is the largest living animal of all, the awe-inspiring blue whale.

But let's start at the beginning, shall we?

Excited to learn more about whales, where they live, how they manage to get so big, and all the amazing characteristics that make them the sensational creatures they are?

Then c'mon, there's no time to waste!

Let's go take a deep, deep dive and meet whales, the most legendary sea creatures of all!

INTERESTING FACT: The oldest known depiction of whales was discovered in Chile – an extraordinary hand-painting in a cave that dates back more than 1,500 years. The rock art depicts whales being hunted, which is a sad but true representation of the relationship between humans and whales. We have hunted them for a very long time, and in some countries, hunting whales is still allowed. This is despite the fact that most of the world has agreed: whales are in danger and should not be hunted for any reason!

WHALE HELLO THERE...

WHAT IS A WHALE?

You may already know that whales are not fish. They are, in fact, **mammals**, just like us humans. Just like us humans, whales breathe in air through their lungs, have hair around their mouths, produce milk when they are pregnant, and give birth to live young. Yet, *unlike* us humans, whales manage to do all that while living at sea. For this reason, alongside dolphins and porpoises, whales are known as **cetaceans**, or *aquatic* mammals, to be more precise.

Cetaceans are one of four distinct species of marine animals, and a few specific traits separate them from other sea-dwelling creatures like sea lions, seals, and walruses. *Can you guess the biggest difference between whales and sea lions, seals and walruses?* If you've watched a lot of marine life documentaries, we bet you can probably guess.

That's right, **whales spend their entire life at sea while the other three species of marine animals actually need to come out of the water regularly.**

How can whales, as mammals, live their whole life at sea?

Because they have **blowholes,** of course!

Blowholes: a whale's most impressive superpower

Whales have blowholes right at the top of their head, and it is through this fascinating bit of anatomy that whales can breathe and still live at sea. When a whale needs to take a breath, it comes up to the surface, blows out water (*there she blows!*), and takes a big breath.

Whales can hold their breath for an impressive amount of time. Some species up to an hour and a half! This, coupled with a serious amount of blubber under their skin, allows them to stay warm, even in the coldest of seas.

FUN FACT: The closest non-cetacean living relative of the whale is the hippopotamus! These two gentle giants are each other's closest relatives and are believed to have shared a common ancestor around 55 MILLION years ago!

Dedicated scientists have been studying whales for decades and what they have discovered is astonishing. Whales are not only highly intelligent, but they also appear to have formed their own regional culture. This means that groups of

whales behave and even communicate differ-
ently, depending on where they come from. Similar to how people of different countries speak
their own unique languages and have their own
distinct traditions.

Pretty awesome, right?

Whales are renowned for being ridiculously
colossal, yet not all whale species are humon-
gous. Sure, the majestic blue whale can grow as
long as three school buses and weigh as much as
150 tons, but he is the king of whales, after all.
The dwarf sperm whale, on the other hand, is

actually smaller than a dolphin. This is the smallest whale species of all and proves that the world of whales is as big as it is varied.

How do whales communicate?

Scientists believe that whales use vocal sounds and body language to communicate with each other, pretty much the way humans do. **Researchers have even discovered that some whales can actually sing!**

Whales are famous for their beautiful songs that can travel long distances under the water. It is a loud noise, much louder than anything humans could ever make. As lovely as it is to think that whales 'sing' like we do, many experts believe the singing might be more than just a recreational pastime. It's highly likely that whales 'sing' to communicate with other whales many miles away.

Amazingly, whales have also been seen playing, much like how you might play ball with your friends. They have been spotted playing with seaweed and other things they find in the water. Researchers think whales play for the same reason many other animals do: *to learn about their*

environment and nurture social bonds with other members of their species.

FUN FACT: Scientists who dedicate their careers to studying whales are called **cetologists** or whale biologists. To become one, you should study animal science in college and gain a Bachelor's Degree in marine biology. Any degree in environmental or natural science will also pave the way for a career as a cetologist!

WHY DO WHALES LIKE SALTWATER?

Pepper makes them sneeze!

TYPES OF WHALES

T he many species of whales are subdivided into two kinds: **toothed whales** and **baleen whales.**

THE LARGEST

THE SMALLEST

THE RAREST

THE MOST COMMON

THE MOST ENTERTAINING

THE WEIRDEST

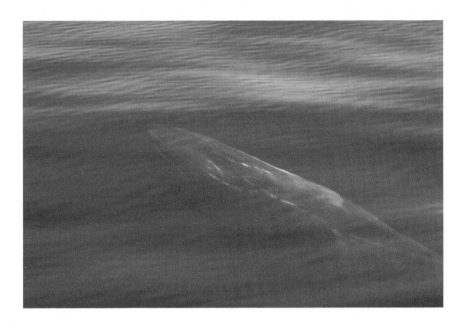

MEET THE TOOTHED WHALES

As their name suggests, toothed whales have teeth! Just like you and us, they have a set of upper and lower teeth that they use to eat their food. They also have powerful jaws that help them to bite down hard on their prey. There are about 76 different kinds of toothed whales, and they are all **apex predators.** That means they eat other animals for food but are not regularly hunted by other animals.

While it may sound like they would be scary, most toothed whales are actually adorable. They include some of the smallest whales, like the 3.5-

foot-long dwarf sperm whale, all the way up to the enormous sperm whale, which can grow up to a whopping 52 feet in length.

Let's meet some fascinating toothed whales, shall we?

SPERM WHALES

Sperm whales are the largest of all the toothed whales. Males usually grow to an average of 52 feet in length and 53 tons in weight. The largest ever recorded of this species measured an incredible 59 feet! Females usually weigh about one-third of the weight of males. They are mostly grey with some white patches on their belly.

Sperm whales got their name from the waxy substance that is found in their heads, which is called **spermaceti**. Once upon a time, sperm whales were hunted for this substance, which people used to make candles, oils, make-up, and other products.

Sperm whales are fascinating because they have the biggest brain of any animal on Earth! In fact, their brains can weigh up to 10 pounds. That's more than three times bigger than a human brain! They have a big square head that makes up for about one-third of their entire body.

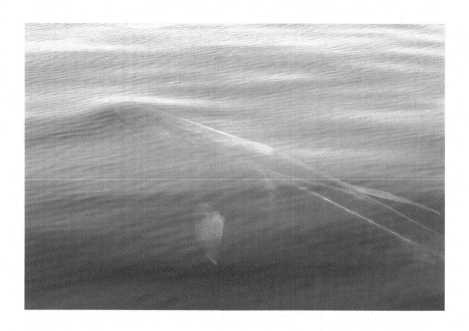

Sperm whales are also good at using **echolocation**. Echolocation is when an animal uses sound to figure out where things are. Sperm whales use echolocation to find their food, which is mostly squid. They use a special kind of sound called a **click**. Clicking sounds are really loud, and they can travel through water for long distances. When the clicks hit something, they make an echo, and that's how the sperm whale knows where its food is.

Boasting one of the widest distributions of all, sperm whales can be spotted all over the world: from North America to Europe, New Zealand, Asia, and even the cold Arctic.

BELUGA WHALES

Beluga whales are much smaller than sperm whales. They only grow to about 15 feet in length and weigh around 3,000 pounds.

Beluga whales are known for their white color. In fact, the word "beluga" means "white" in Russian. *Did you know that baby belugas are actually born gray?* It takes them a few years to turn completely white.

Beluga whales are also known for their big, round heads and for being one of the most vocal whale species of all. Experts call them the '*canaries of the sea*' because they love to talk and sing so much!

Beluga whales live in Arctic and sub-Arctic waters. That means it's really cold where they live, and the water is usually covered in ice. But don't worry, beluga whales are built for cold weather. They have a layer of blubber that keeps them warm, and they also have something else that helps them to survive in the cold — **unique**

blood vessels. These vessels help keep their blood from getting too cold.

A hungry beluga can chow down on about 60 pounds of food every single day. They absolutely love cod, herring, and salmon, as well as octopuses, crabs, squid, and many other sea creatures.

MEET THE BALEEN WHALES

Baleen whales are a bit different from toothed whales: they don't have teeth but, instead, have what scientists call baleen plates. These are made of a special material called *keratin*, which is what our fingernails are made of! The plates hang down from the top of their mouths, and they use them to filter food out of the water. They swim with their mouths open and take in a lot of water. Then they push the water back out, and all the tiny animals they want to eat are caught in the baleen plates, so they can just swallow them whole.

Usually, baleen whales eat very small fish and tiny organisms like krill, algae, and plankton. They use their baleen plates like you might use a strainer when you boil vegetables or spaghetti. The water goes, and the food stays!

Now that's a neat trick, wouldn't you say?

Baleen whales are the largest animals on our planet, so they are also the largest of all whale species. Unlike many toothed whales who prefer to live in pods, baleen whales tend to be solitary animals. This means they live alone and only come together during mating season.

FUN FACT: Marine biologists call baleen whales the *'vigilantes of the sea'* because they live alone and are known to protect other sea animals (*like dolphins*) from attacks (*usually by sharks*). Although they are not exceptionally sociable or friendly, they have never been known to be aggressive. Unless, of course, they want to protect a threatened sea animal!

Found in every ocean all over the planet, baleen whales have huge tail flukes, which they use like paddles to swim very great distances. Most baleen whales are pretty dark (*usually grey or black*) with lighter shades on their underbelly. The easiest way to spot them out at sea is by their darker coloring.

All up, there are 12 distinct sub-species of baleen whales, and they can range in length from 20 up to 120 feet.

BLUE WHALES

The blue whale is not only the most enormous whale of all, but it is also the most giant animal that has *ever* lived on Earth. That's right, bigger than any of the dinosaurs that existed! The biggest one ever found was over 98 feet long and weighed over 199 tons!

Can you imagine how much food it must take to feed a whale that big? Well, we'll find that out later, and we're sure you'll be surprised!

When they are born, baby blue whales are already about 23 feet long and weigh about 5,500 pounds. **AT BIRTH! Isn't that crazy??**

That's longer than three fully grown humans stacked on top of one another and much, much heavier too. A nursing mother can produce over 50 gallons of milk a day for her newborn baby blue. In contrast, adults in North America consume about 17 gallons of milk per YEAR.

Unsurprisingly, baby blue whales can easily gain up to 200 pounds daily.

No kidding?!

VAQUITA WHALES

On the opposite end of the size spectrum is where you'll find the vaquita, the smallest baleen species and actually the smallest, rarest, and most endangered whale of all.

The vaquita grows to merely five feet in length and is found only in the Gulf of California. They are dark grey in color, with black rings around their eyes and dark patches on their mouth.

Unfortunately, due to their diminutive size, vaquitas often get caught in fishing nets, where they can easily drown. This is considered the most endangered marine species on our planet. Although they may look like porpoises, vaquitas are closer to whales than dolphins.

FIN WHALES

Fin whales are the second largest animal on Earth, after the blue whale. They can grow to be about 85 feet long and weigh around 200,000 pounds. They can live up to 80 and even 90 years if left undisturbed.

Fin whales were named after their big fins, but they are also known for their long necks and small heads.

In fact, their heads are so small that they can barely fit their brains inside! But even though their heads are small, they still have enormous mouths. In fact, their mouths can be up to 15 feet wide, and their tongues can weigh as much as an elephant!

Can you imagine having a tongue that weighed as much as an elephant?

These **fin-tastic** creatures were sadly hunted a lot in the 1900s, and now experts believe there are only 100,000 left in our seas. They can be seen almost all over the world, although they prefer the Indian, Pacific, and Antarctic oceans.

Because they can live in various regions of the world, the fin whale's diet can be varied and heavily depends on where they are. Surely that makes them very happy because who doesn't like variety in their diet?

OMURA'S WHALE

Did you know that there was a kind of whale that was only discovered in the last few years? **It's true!** Omura's whale was only identified as a different species in 2003. Before then, they were thought to be a smaller type of fin whale because they look very much alike and live in similar regions of the world. Genetic testing has since confirmed that Omura's are more closely related to blue whales.

Mind you, it's hard to see the connection, given that Omura's are pretty small. They only grow to be about 33 feet in length — *which is still pretty big compared to other animals.* And that's not the only thing that makes them special. They also have something pretty rare — **blue eyes!**

Omura's whales are found in tropical and subtropical waters all over the world. And because they live in warm waters, they don't have a lot of blubber. They are primarily blue, but they can also be white or gray. And they have long, thin fins. In fact, their fins are so long and thin that they look more like wings than fins!

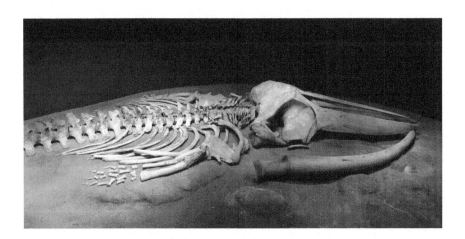

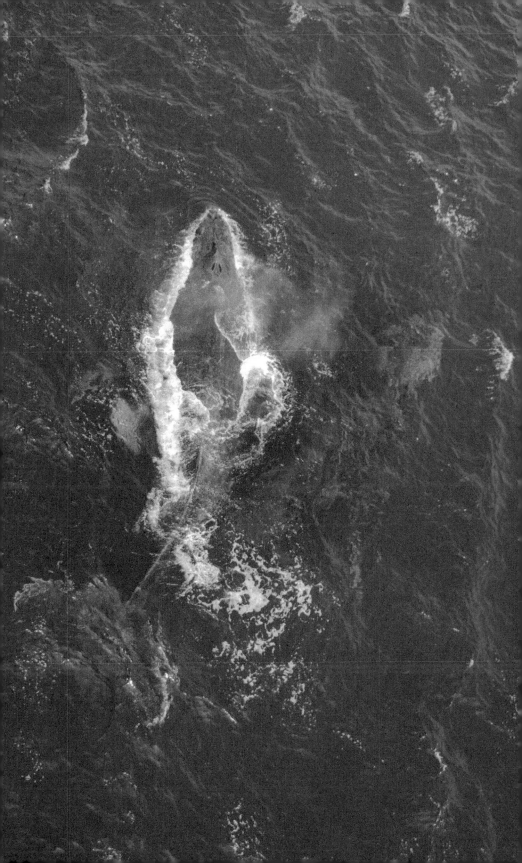

WHAT DO WHALES NEED TO STAY HEALTHY?

Vitamin SEA!

THE HISTORY OF WHALES

Now that you know a little bit more about these fascinating creatures, let's take a look at their history and how they came to be the whales we know today. Whales are believed to have originated from land mammals that lived in Asia during the Jurassic period. *That's a **long** time ago!*

During this time, the world was a very different place. The land was lush and green, with many rivers and lakes. The air was thick with humidity, and the climate was warm. Asia was home to some of the largest animals that have ever lived on Earth, including dinosaurs! These early whales were small, had four legs, and could swim and walk on land. Over time, they began to lose their hind limbs and became better adapted to life at sea.

As they continued to evolve, whales began to look more and more like the creatures we know today. Their front limbs transformed into flippers and their bodies became long and smooth, making them ideally suited for life in the ocean.

Over the years, humans have hunted whales for their meat, oil, and blubber. This has led to a drastic decline in many whale populations. However, thanks to conservation efforts, some species of whales are beginning to rebound. These magnificent creatures must be protected so that future generations can enjoy their existence as well.

WHERE **TH**ERE'S A WHALE,

THERE'S A WAY!

WHERE TO GO WHALE WATCHING

Different whale species prefer to live in certain regions of our world's oceans. Some are better suited to cold water, so you will find them near the north and south poles, while others prefer much warmer seas, the kind you find around the tropics.

Most toothed whales live in **pods**, which are *groups that can have from 12 up to 40 members*. Seeing a pod of whales on a whale-watching boat trip is one of the most magical travel experiences you could ever have.

The best destination to see whales are down in Baja California (Mexico), Hudson Bay (Canada),

Hervey Bay (Australia), and the Antarctic Peninsula, among many others.

When planning a whale-watching trip, you will want to research the migration habits of whales. Certain places and months of the year are better for spotting a specific whale. For example, you might want to travel to the Dominican Republic to see humpback whales in the weeks between January and March. These gracious giants travel there during the winter because the seas are much warmer.

Whale-watching trips are very popular all over the world. If you are a lover of whales, you might want to travel all over the world when you are grown up just to see all the different species of whales.

Now wouldn't that be a marvelous plan?

FUN FACT: As you know, the world is made up of land and sea. What you might not know is that there is far more water than land – in fact, more than two-thirds of our planet is covered in water. Surprisingly, over 80% of all animal species live on land, which means just 20% live in our oceans, seas, rivers, and lakes.

WHERE DO WHALES SLEEP AT BEDTIME?

In water beds!

THE LIFE CYCLE OF WHALES

All creatures have a life cycle, and whales are no different. Just like us, they are born, they grow up, and they die. But there are some differences between a human's life cycle and a whale's life cycle. Let's take a closer look at the life cycle of whales and see how they grow and change as they get older. *Are you ready to learn more?*

The first stage of a whale's life cycle is when they are born. Baby whales are called **calves**, and they're born alive (*not in an egg!*), just like human babies. But there are some differences.

For one thing, baby whales are born in the water, not on land like human babies. Because of this major difference, whales are born tail first. This is so they can start swimming as soon as their heads pop out, and it also prevents them from drowning if the last part of the delivery takes a long time. Human babies, however, are born head first. This is so they can start breathing even before they are fully delivered in case full delivery is delayed.

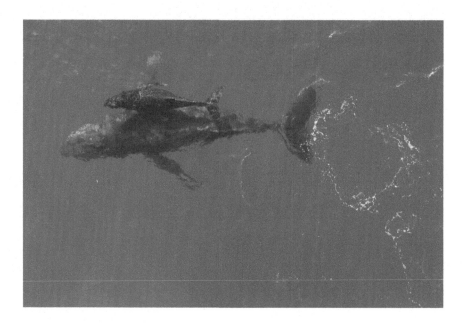

Baby whales are already born with a healthy layer of blubber, which helps keep them warm in cold water from the very first moment it is born. Blubber also helps whale calves float until they learn how to swim on their own.

After a baby whale is born, it starts to grow very quickly and actually continues to grow for years. A whale is considered an adult when it is about eight years old.

During this time, the baby whale also learns how to swim and hunt for food. It's a lot to learn, but they have their parents to help them. Once they've learned everything they need to know, they're ready to start their own family and have babies of their own.

Of all the whale species, the bowhead whale boasts the longest lifespan. Experts believe these incredible creatures can live up to **200** years of age. The gin whale comes a close second. The oldest ever recorded was a 140-year-old senior!

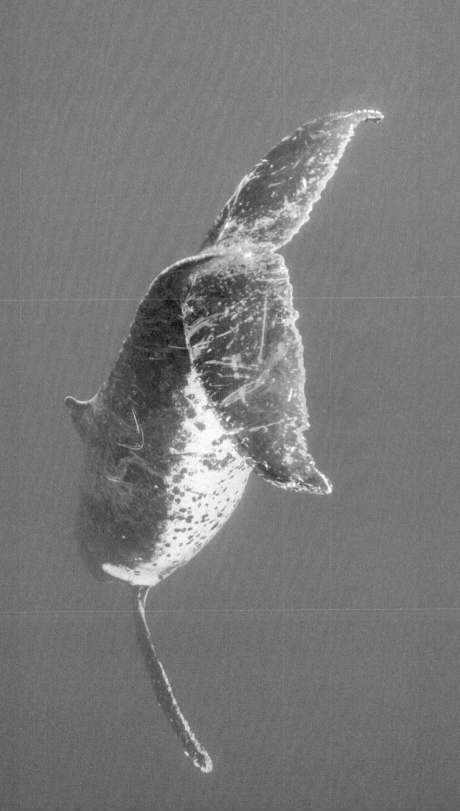

WE **THINK** YOU'RE JUST S'WHALE!

SUPER COOL WHALE FACTS

By now, you know that whales come in all sorts of shapes and varying shades of grey and black. What might surprise you is that they actually don't eat that much, considering their size.

A WHALE OF A FEAST!

A blue whale eats about four tons of food per day. That might sound like a lot, but it's actually only about 1% of its body weight. So if you weigh 100 pounds, that would be like you eating one pound of food per day, which isn't all that much!

QUALITY OF FOOD MATTERS...*A LOT!*

What is amazing is knowing that even the tiniest sea creatures, like krill, contain all the nutrients whales need to grow strong and colossal. Four tons of krill every single day is what a giant whale needs to survive. Krill is also a fantastic source of energy, which is vital for whales because they use a lot of energy when they swim.

WHALES ARE *BIG* HEARTED ANIMALS

Whales have a four-chambered heart. In fact, all mammals have a four-chambered heart. *But did you know that whales have the biggest four-chambered heart of all?* **That's right!** The average whale heart is the size of a human adult and can weigh up to 400 pounds! Can you imagine how big that is? And how strong its pump must be to circulate all that blood?

GETTING SOME ZZZZZZ'S

Whales have been observed sleeping in two different ways. They either rest completely in the water, either vertically or horizontally! In other cases, they sleep while swimming very slowly next to another sea animal. Well, that's their way of avoiding predators!

FATTY MILK MAKES WHALES BIG AND STRONG

Like all mammals, female whales produce milk to feed their young. But the composition of whale milk is quite different from human milk. For one thing, it's much higher in fat, which helps keep the baby warm in the cold ocean water. And another difference is that it contains more protein, which helps the baby grow quickly.

TWO-OF-A-KIND

Having twins is super rare for whales, and only about 1% of all cetacean births are thought to be twins. But it does occasionally happen!

WHALES CAN BE BIG SOFTIES

Calves usually drink milk from their mothers for several months, but scientists have discovered that some are big softies and will continue to suckle on their mothers long after she no longer makes milk.

WHALES FART JUST LIKE YOU!

When whales eat a lot of food, they produce a lot of gas. And just like us, that gas has to go *somewhere*! So, whales fart out the gas through their blowholes. And if that's not crazy enough, a blue whale's fart bubble is large enough to enclose a small horse! But don't worry, their farts don't smell bad because the gas is mostly water vapor.

Thank goodness...

EVER**YTHING**
WHA**LE** BE OKAY!

HELP WHALES SURVIVE!

By being interested in whales and learning more about them, you are already helping whales survive. **Yes, it's true!** Just by learning about these fantastic creatures and spreading the amazing facts you have learned, you're helping protect them. **Because the more we know about something, the more we care about it.**

"*Thank you for your concern!*" That's from a whale in every ocean! Know that they are very grateful for your care and consciousness. By showing your concern and wanting to know more about them, you are part of the solution to solving some of the problems they currently face.

Many whale species are endangered and vulnerable, and they need your help to keep them safe. You can help by learning about the threats they face and what you can do to reduce them.

One of the biggest threats to whales is something called "whaling." Whaling is the hunting of whales for their meat, oil, and other body parts. It's a problem because it reduces the number of whales in the ocean, which can cause them to become extinct.

We need your help to stop whaling! You can make a difference by raising awareness about this issue by telling your friends and family about it. Every voice counts, and together, we can make a difference!

There are other things you can do to help whales, such as:

- Support organizations that are working to protect them. You can save your extra allowance, do chores around the house, or have a lemonade stand and donate the money to groups that give importance to whales.
- Share your knowledge with your friends about the importance of preserving these majestic creatures. You can also share with them this fun book about whales! They'll definitely love it and learn a lot from it.

I THINK WHALE MAKE A GREAT TEAM!

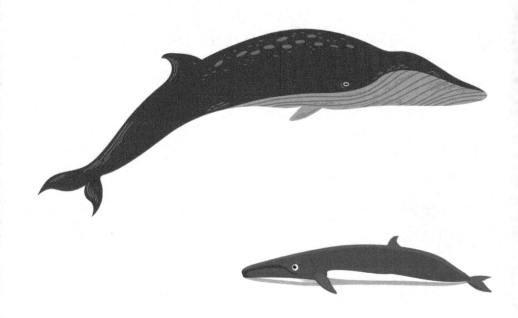

THANK YOU!

T hank you for reading this book and for allowing us to share our love for whales with you!

If you've enjoyed this book, please let us know by leaving a rating and a brief review wherever you made your purchase! This helps us spread the word to other readers!

Thank you for your time, and have an awesome day!

For more information, please visit:

www.animalreads.com

SEA YOU LATER!

Made in the USA
Coppell, TX
18 August 2023

20500967R00044